Jewel
How I found little Angel
Adventurous story
Part 2

By
Mercedes Monden

Jewel

How I found little Angel

© 2017 Mercedes Monden

ISBN 13: 9789081784368
ISBN 10: 90-817843-6-6
Printed by CreateSpace, an Amazon.com Company.
Available from Amazon.com and other retail outlets.
All rights reserved. No part of this publication may be reproduced or transmitted in any form or by any means, electronic or mechanical, including photocopy, recording, or any information storage retrieval system, without permission in writing from the copyright owner.

About Jewel
How I found little Angel" Part 2,

This book is an adventurous, and inspirational faith base fun read book; for children between the ages of 6 to 12. in this book, kids learn the helping others in need; courage, care, faith and adventure in a fun way

One day, Jewel was walking to the corner shop to pick something up for her mother. As she walked by the dump, she saw a small figure dressed in brown and yellow,

walking along and picking things up. She stopped to take a close look at the figure; it was a child; who was perhaps about 6 years old. She saw Jewel and ran away with her sack full of junk.

The next day, she was at the dump again, and as soon as she saw Jewel, she ran away. This went on for a while; she never stayed long enough for Jewel to talk to her. Jewel wondered if she had a home.

One day, after seeing this girl for two weeks, Jewel followed her to see where she went. She didn't go to the row of houses and apartment buildings where almost everyone lived; instead, she ran through the cornfield and kept going, heading through the woods.

Jewel got frightened as it was getting dark. Jewel followed her until she saw a large house. It was a dull brown colour and had broken bricks falling out of it everywhere. Jewel ran home through the woods and the cornfield as fast as she could.

That night, Jewel dreamt that she was afraid of a dark room, but she didn't know why.

The next day, she went to the house to see if she could find out more about the girl. After breakfast, Jewel told her mum she was going to a friend's house; a new friend because she wanted to be friends with the girl - even though she looked like she was about 6 years younger than Jewel.

Jewel walked through the path the girl had made by walking through the cornfield every day. As Jewel arrived at the house, it became freezing. Jewel put on her jacket and tiptoed up to the house.

She peeked into the window and saw the girl standing in front of an old woman. Jewel could hear what they were saying.

"Aunty," the girl said, "give me my locket back. I found it!"

"You shall not get it back," snapped the person she called aunty, "It is mine

now. It has gone to the basement with all your other treasures. You must treasure nothing!"

The girl cried, then ran out of the house. She saw Jewel. Jewel held out her arms and said,

"Are you okay?" She held Jewel"s hand all the way to her apartment. She was still shaking when they got there.

Jewel felt so bad that the little girl had lost her locket, and Jewel remembered the locket her friend, Lia, had given her 4 years ago. Jewel had never worn it, so she gave it to the little girl.

Jewel told her mother she was taking care of the girl while her Aunt was running an errand. They went to Jewel's bedroom, and Jewel asked her what her name was.

"Angel," she replied in a small, frightened voice.

"It's okay, don't be frightened," Jewel replied in a calm voice. The little girl jumped up onto Jewel"s bed and lay down. Jewel told her that she had a surprise for her.

"Really?" she said full of hope, "No one has ever given me anything before!" Jewel was surprised.

"What about your dress?" Jewel asked her.

"I found it in the dump all ripped up, and I sewed it."

That was it. This precious girl was not properly cared for, and she wore clothes that had been thrown away! Jewel felt a sudden need to take care of the girl herself, but she knew her Aunt would not approve.

All of a sudden, the little girl jumped off the bed and said, "I have to go now!" Jewel was surprised.

"Don't you want to stay? And what"s your name?" Jewel asked her name again.

"Angel, and yes," she answered, "but I can't. You see, my Aunt will be terribly mad, and she will make me stay in the basement! It's dark in there!"

Jewel was even more shocked when she heard this.

Why would anyone lock up a child in a dark basement? Jewel had a strange feeling that this woman was not Angel's relative. She walked her home and told the little girl that she would give her the surprise when she saw her next. Angel went inside the house with a sad wave. Jewel hoped her Aunt wouldn't be too mad at her.

The next day, Jewel ran to Angel's house. The little girl was just coming out of her house with a dirty pillowcase. Jewel had the locket tucked away in her pocket. They walked to the dump and Jewel helped her look for things that were still good. She told Jewel that her mother was a "Collector." Jewel thought it was pretty strange.

Jewel gave Angel the locket, and she jumped for joy. She said she couldn't take it home. Jewel thought she didn't want it. Jewel puts it around Angel"s neck anyway, and she hugged Jewel.

The next day, they went back to the dump, and she didn't have her locket on. "Where's the locket I gave to you?" Jewel asked her.

"In my hiding spot," she replied. At this moment, Jewel was so overloaded with questions to ask Angel that her head was buzzing.

That night, Jewel had a horrible nightmare that Angel was locked in her basement and she couldn't get out. Jewel woke up in a cold sweat. The last time Jewel had dreamt about Angel the dream had come true! At least, it was real before she dreamt it. Jewel looked at the clock. It was only 3:30 AM. Jewel remembered what her mommy said to her; ""Read your scriptures and pray in your Heavenly language until you fall back to sleep; remember The Lord gives sleep to His love ones"" Jewel read until 6:30 because she couldn't get back to

sleep. Jewel did read through Psalm 91; she prayed for Angel too, believing God to rescue her; Jewel could not stop thinking about Angel.

"Is she really locked in the basement?" Jewel asked herself quietly. Oh no! Another question! How was she ever going to find out all the answers? Jewel decided to go to Angel's house right away to see if Angel could answer any of her questions

Jewel left the house very quietly so she wouldn't wake her parents. She crept through the cornfield and into the woods until she came to the spooky house. She peeked in the window and saw Angel's Aunt yelling at her.

"You are a bad girl, give me that locket!" she snapped.

"But this one's mine! I got it from my friend!" Angel insisted.

Jewel felt like running into the house and yelling at that woman. She had given the locket to Angel! Jewel kept watching as Angel's "Aunt" broke off Angel's necklace and put it in her pocket. That's when Angel burst out,

"I don't like you. You are ungrateful, and you don't love me. Jewel loves me!" That's when Jewel began to cry. Jewel really did love her like a little sister.

Then, that wretched woman pushed Angel as hard as she could into the open basement door. Jewel could hear her screaming as she fell down the stairs into the darkness below.

Jewel ran home, sobbing, and called 112.

"Police, fire, or medical please," the dispatcher asked. "Medical," she answered in a shaky voice.

"Address?" he asked.

"577 West HighPraise Avenue," Jewel answered. Jewel had given the dispatcher her address. Jewel didn't know Angel's address, and she wasn't sure if the ambulance could get to her house.

When the ambulance arrived Jewel told the paramedics to follow her. They followed Jewel through the cornfield, and through the woods. When they got to the house, Jewel opened the door. Before Jewel had left, she saw the Aunt ran out of the house. She ran in the opposite direction of Jewel"s house and the dump, so Jewel was sure she hadn't seen the ambulance.

Jewel ran to the basement door. It was locked with a key. Jewel had seen an axe by the window where she had been looking in, so she ran out and grabbed it. She then ran back in and hacked the door open. Jewel felt around for the light switch, but there wasn't one.

"Do you have a flashlight?" Jewel asked frantically. One of the paramedics just happened to have a long flashlight. Jewel grabbed it from him and ran down the stairs. When she got to the bottom, Jewel saw Angel"s limp body lying on the concrete floor.

"Oh my God," Jewel whispered to myself while she began to cry, "is she dead?" The paramedics checked for a pulse and if she was breathing.

"She has a heartbeat, but her breathing is very shallow," one of the paramedics said, "She may have broken some bones, but chances are she'll be all right." After a short silence, she asked, "What's her name was?"

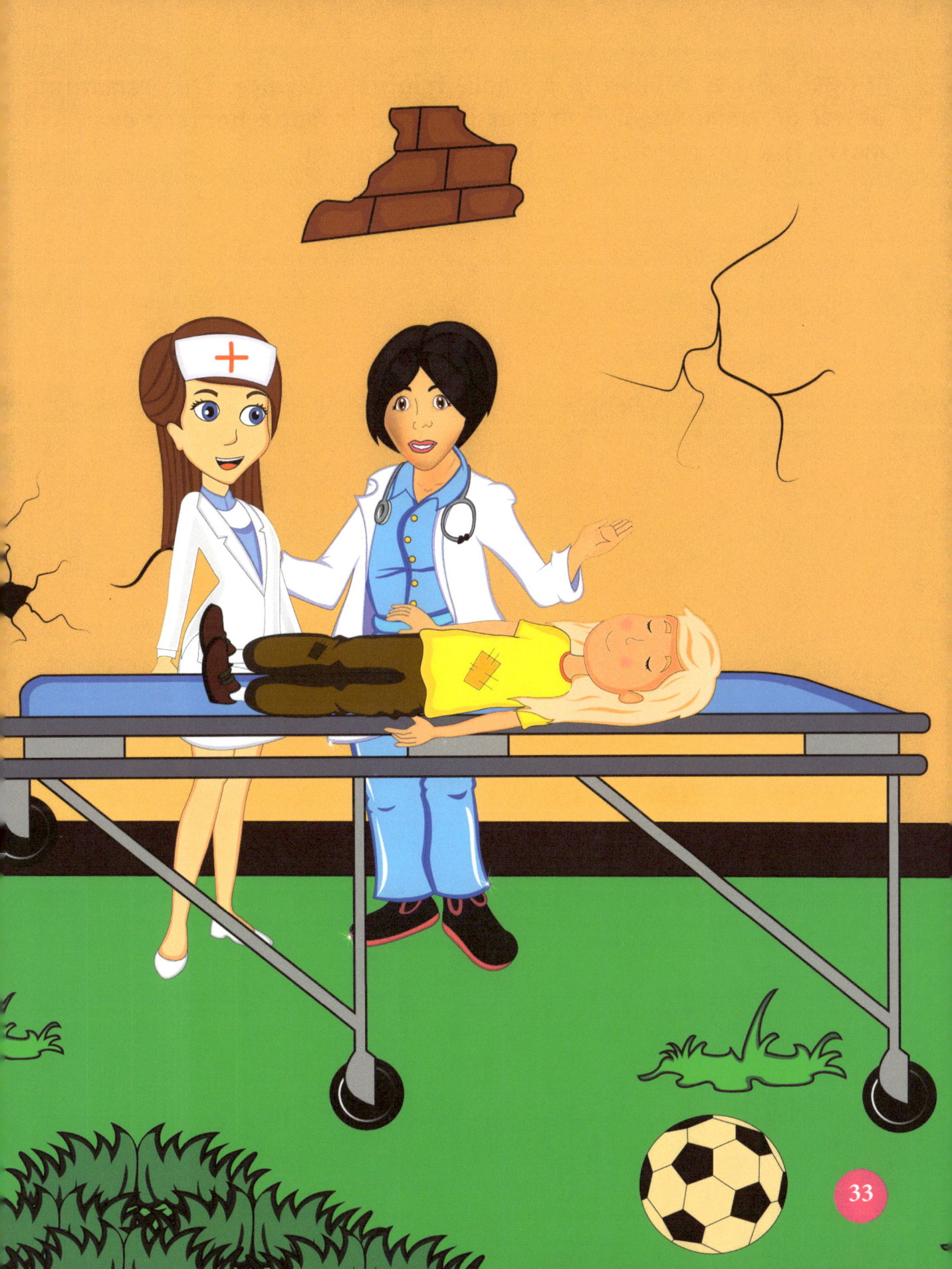

"Angel," Jewel replied in a small, frightened voice. This reminded Jewel of when Angel first met her, and it made her cry even more. The paramedics told her to calm down.

"we need to run medical checkup on at the emergency room, come with us... what's your name?"

"I am Jewel," with another sob.

"I am proud of you; for saving Angel's life by calling authorities, we are about to head to the hospital, do you want to drive along and Let's call your parents; You must get rest." She replied, saying,

They went back to their vehicle for the stretcher which they lifted Angel onto. Jewel heard a faint whimper as she pulled up the stairs, through the woods and through the cornfield into the ambulance.

Jewel's mum arrived on time to pick her up, but dear are you, all right? you look quiet tired;

Jewel couldn't take it anymore, and she fell asleep with a bear on her hands, special gift she had picked up for little Angel

Later, when she woke up, she couldn't figure out where she was. Jewel looked around and found she was in a hospital room, Angels room with her mum.

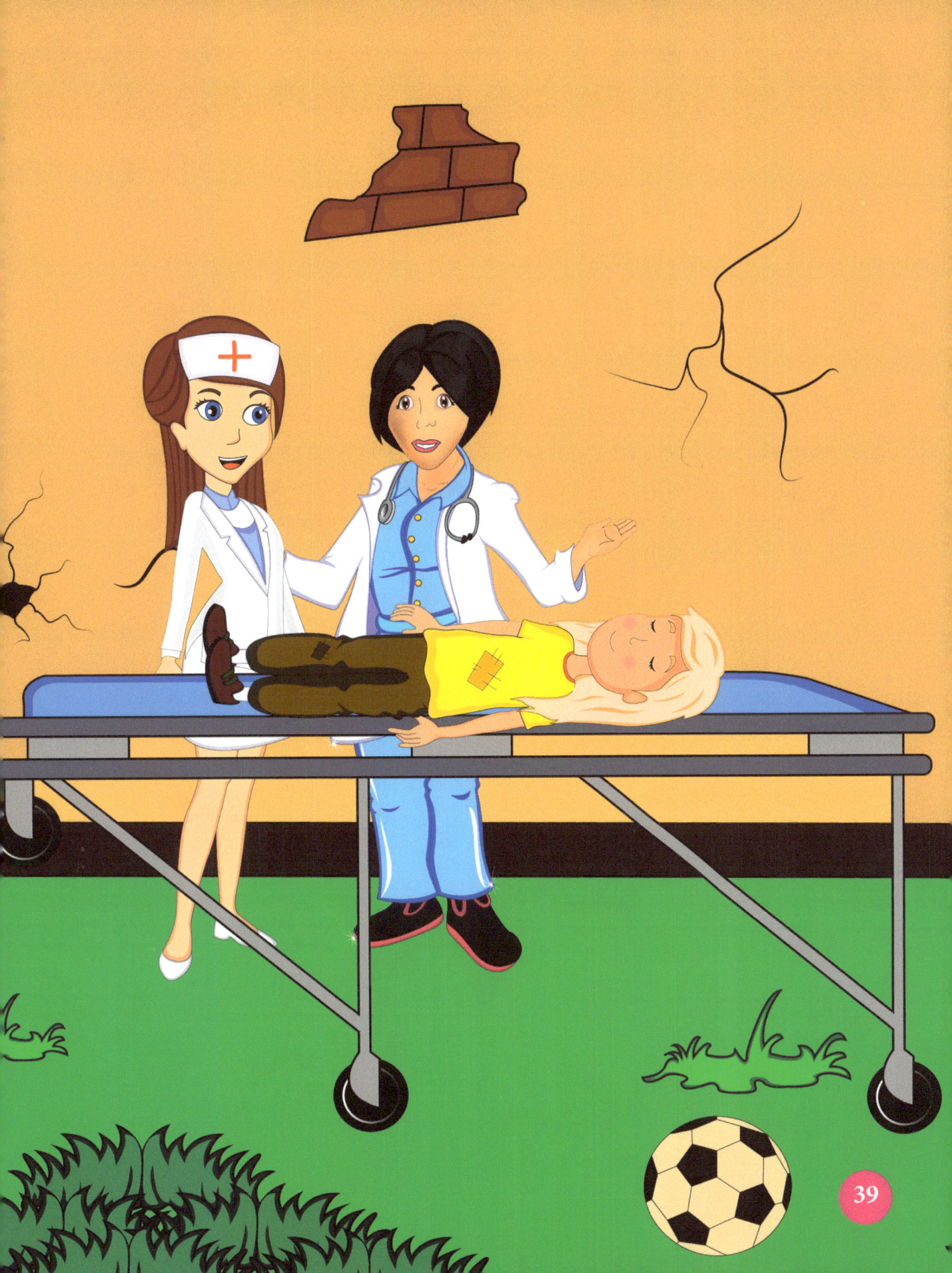

Jewel gaze at emergency hallway from Angels room and she smiled at her little friend when she realises she was at Angels's room. Jewel stood up to go over to the bed and winced as a sharp pain flew up her leg and up her spine. she sat back down.

They carried Jewel to Angels room. Jewel told the medical caregiver about the discomfort she experienced when she moves her legs. The nurse examined her until she found where it hurt.

"Ow!" Jewel yelled when she touched the spot.

"You may have broken your leg, young lady," the nurse replied. "We need to schedule you an x-ray. What's your name?" "Jewel`

The nurse wrote her name on a folder and left. Another nurse came in and examine Angel, then she left. the head doctor came in with a wheelchair.

"Hop in and we'll go to the x-ray room."

Jewel stumbled to the wheelchair. The doctor wheeled her down the hall to a room marked "x-ray." They went in and he told Jewel to lay on the table. She got up, and then another doctor came and put a heavy blanket on her abdomen and asked which leg hurt.

"My right," Jewel replied. He took another heavy blanket and put it on her left leg and wore some sunglasses and put a machine over her leg. He flipped a switch, then there was a bright flash of light. It was over.

The doctor took the blankets off and went to develop the x-ray. Jewel hopped back into the wheelchair and the nurse peeked in and said she could go back to Angel.

"What is the room number please?" Jewel asked.

"277," the nurse replied. Jewel pushed herself along and went back to the room. Angel was sitting up. Jewel wheeled over to the bed and reached for her hand. She held on tight to Jewel's hand.

"how did you hurt yourself?" Angel asked in a small voice.

"I fell out on the floor out of exhaustion on the way here," Jewel replied. "I may have broken my leg."

"That's horrible!" Angel gasped, "I broke both my legs and my right arm." "Are you okay?" Jewel asked.

"Yes, it doesn't hurt anymore." a nurse came in and said,

" you need a cast." She pushed Jewel to the room where her cast would be on. They took her in and wrapped the first soft layer around her leg.

"What colour outside would you like?" the nurse asked.

"yellow please," Jewel replied, thinking about people signing it.

I am so glad we are ok, it's almost like a movie, Angel; I am about to go home,

You will stay with foster parents for a while. mum wants you to come stay with us. but we may not do that without the lawyers

help, mum need to get the right informations on how you can come stay with us; what do you think?

Angel replied with a big smile; I can not wait to have a new family!. I will go to school just like you. and we can go travel around the world!. learn new languages, go on fishing, just like you and Lia, have my room and get clean cloths!

Okay, okay! Jewel replied with a big smile. I hear you. Goodbye, for now, I will come visit you soon. Remember the prayer I taught you?

While Angel started praying; (Jewel Remembered the very first time she ment little Angel)

"Lord Jesus, Angel prayed. when I am afraid, you are there for me. Your Holy Angels protects me. I am loved by You, I am part of Your Family, I am a daughter of the king, I am brilliant, I am

intelligent, I am beautiful and I can do all things because you make me strong! hihihi; I feel better already "Angel said;

"You are intelligent. Remember; fear is not an option, Lets do the pinky goodbye" both girls gigling "We believe in the invincible Being, He believes in us, therefore we believe in ourself; While the girls where playing, the phone rang, its mums phone, "good news girls", what is it, mum? Jewel asked mum; what is it? Angel can come home with us. mum said; for only 6 months, she may stay forever if she wants to, but I need to call your dad to share the great news too!

Jewel and little Angel went back home with mum, I wonder what my next adventure will be like. "Smiling"

Dedication

I dedicate this book to every little child out there; precious children whose parents or friends have gone through a divorce or still dealing with divorced parents. May God strengthen you always and may He heal your broken heart. Remember, you are not here by accident or by chance; God has a special purpose for your life, and I am praying for you.

Acknowledgement

I would like to express my gratitude to the many people who saw me through this book; to all those who provided support, talked things over, read, wrote, offered comments, remarks, and assisted in the editing, proofreading, and design. I would like to thank my husband, John, and my precious daughters, Jewel Glory and Jaylinn Grace, for motivating and enabling me to publish this book to the worldwide web. Above all, I would like to give thanks to my Lord Jesus Christ for always inspiring me to fulfill my purpose. Special thanks to my editor, David, and my illustrator, Arsalan, as well. May God bless you all!

56

www.ingramcontent.com/pod-product-compliance
Lightning Source LLC
Chambersburg PA
CBHW041533040426
42446CB00002B/77